A Very Special Me

This book is dedicated to Grandma Max Rengert, as well as
Dr. Bassem Dahman and the St. John Detroit Medical Staff.
A special thanks to James Steffen for being an amazing daddy and friend.

Created by: Kim Steffen
Written by: Kristin and Todd Wicks
Illustrated by: Emily Marino

Copyright 2011, KAS-Publishing.
35339 23 Mile Rd, P.O. Box 593
New Baltimore, MI 48047

No part of this publication may be reproduced in whole or in part, without written permission of the publisher.
First printing: October 2011. Printed in the United States of America, R.J. Communications – New York, NY, Batch 1011.

Library of Congress Control Number: 2011917660   ISBN 9780578093697

All babies are special,
but if you must know,

I was born just a little more special than most.

On the day I was born,
I was cute but quite little.

Ten fingers, ten toes,
but something different
in my middle.

On my belly,
where my button would be,
were some organs that should
have stayed inside of me!

(In case you don't know,
organs help you go potty.
They digest your food and
take care of your body.)

Lots of doctors were there
to help me get strong.

They put my organs inside me,
back where they belong.

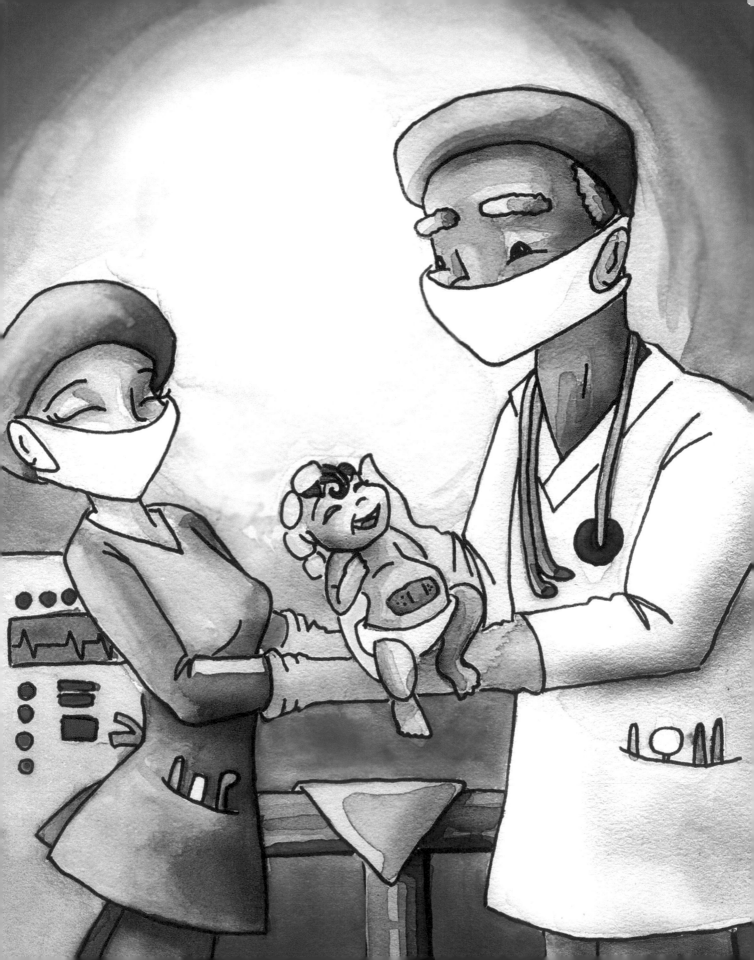

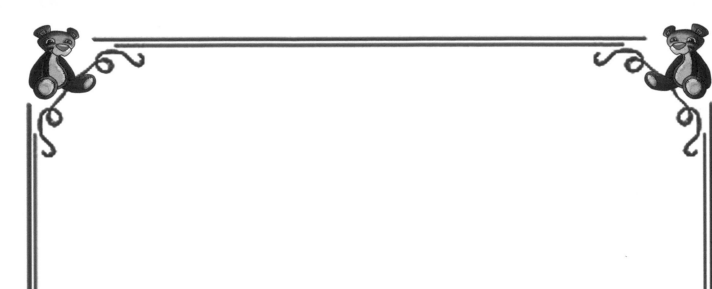

I stayed in the hospital
for a few weeks to mend.

But I wasn't scared,
I made lots of new friends!

*T*here were doctors and nurses
and others who cared.

And uncles and aunts
who kept me in their prayers.

It was easy to heal, 'cause I knew I was blessed.

God watched over me, while I got lots of rest.

W hen I was all better,
Mom and Dad took me home.

And they tell me each day,
so I always know. . .

"We're happy you're
growing and healthy inside.

You are special to us —
you're one of a kind!"

Brianna's Story
Through Her Mommy's Eyes

On January 30, 2006, at a routine ultrasound, we discovered our daughter Brianna had an omphalocele containing her liver, stomach, gallbladder and small and large intestines. After the ultrasound, an amniocentesis took place to determine the fate of our daughter. Two long weeks later, the results confirmed her omphalocele was an isolated condition.

On June 19, 2006, my water broke and our little 6 lb., 1 oz. bundle of joy was born via C-section. She entered the world with a loud scream that quickly ended because the protective sac over her organs ruptured and she was immediately taken to surgery. Her daddy saw her for a few seconds prior to her surgery, but I had to wait eight long hours before seeing my baby's face. My first thought was, "She's perfect and I won't leave her side until her booboo is better!"

During the first few weeks of Brianna's life, she went through many reductions and three major surgeries. There were many times we worried about her outcome, but her little body managed to fight through each of the surgeries. Luckily, our little fighter had no other problems and recovered quickly.

On July 25, 2006, we were able to take her home! At home, Brianna struggled with her feedings as well as severe reflux. Because she was vented so early, she had to learn to drink from a bottle. Her first encounter putting anything down her throat was painful, and her abdominal surgeries made eating very unappealing. If she had too much, she would get sick and not want to eat; therefore, we had to keep her from eating too fast, and then stop her after a certain amount. The challenge was we still needed to meet the required amount of ounces for the day. With a lot of dedication, Brianna miraculously stopped having feeding and reflux issues by age two!

Brianna's abdomen was small because it never expanded in the womb to accommodate her developing organs. Because of this, doctors had a difficult time fully closing her abdomen muscles during early surgeries. On April 12, 2010, her muscles were successfully closed with the support of a Gore-Tex patch. Prior to this surgery, Brianna asked a lot of questions. A nurse suggested a kids' book that could help her understand what was going to happen. Because I couldn't find the right book for this situation or age, I decided to write one myself. Through a support group, I met Emily, an artist who is also an omphalocele adult. Emily was able to take the words provided and easily put emotions and life experiences into her pictures, bringing them beautifully to life.

Brianna loves to hear the story of how her tummy made her special. When she was younger, she used to show others her tummy, so they knew just how special she was, too!

Emily's Story
A Look at the Artist

On November 23, 1982, Emily was born in Orlando, Florida, with a large omphalocele containing her intestines, liver and spleen. Her mother gave birth to her naturally and was unaware of her omphalocele until she was born.

Emily's mother didn't even get to hold her first newborn, as she was quickly whisked away to intensive care at a nearby specialty hospital, where she was given a 10% chance of survival. Over the next 10 days, Emily underwent the slow reintroduction of her organs. On the 10th day, Emily had her closure surgery and immediately went into heart and lung failure due to the stress on her body. It took doctors and specialists seven minutes to bring her back to life. Emily stayed in the hospital for over a month, but was finally released on Christmas Eve after her parents begged doctors to let her come home for the holidays.

Emily beat the odds thanks to the knowledge, meticulous care and compassion of Orlando's first board-certified pediatric surgeon, Dr. Ronald F. David. Once out of the hospital, Emily spent the first year of her life on a heart and lung monitor, but continued to gain strength and heal. Thanks to Dr. David and her parents' love, hope and devotion, Emily continued to grow stronger and thrive.

Today, Emily is healthy. She works as a professional illustrator and is also finishing school to become a doctor of veterinary medicine. She resides in Broomfield, Colorado, with her partner, Andrew, and her dogs, Max and Mischa.

What is an Omphalocele?

An omphalocele develops as a baby grows inside its mother's womb. The muscles in the abdominal wall (umbilical ring) do not close properly, and as a result, the intestines remain outside the umbilical cord. The omphalocele can be small, with only a small loop of intestines present outside the abdomen, or large, containing most of the abdominal organs. In severe cases, surgical treatment is more difficult because the infant's abdomen is abnormally small because it had no need to expand to accommodate the developing organs.

Approximately 30% of babies have a chromosomal (genetic) abnormality, while more than half have abnormalities of other organs or body parts — most commonly the spine, digestive system, heart, urinary system and limbs. Infants with an omphalocele may experience GI tract problems such as feeding difficulties, bowel obstruction and gastroesophageal reflux. A small omphalocele occurs in one out of every 5,000 live births and a large omphalocele (involving the intestines, liver and other organs) occurs in one out of every 10,000 live births.

Brianna, 5 hours old

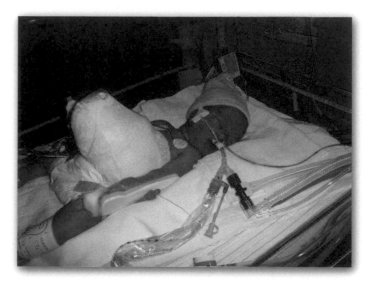

For more information, visit www.omphalocele.net.
Profits from this book will be donated to omphalocele causes.

CPSIA information can be obtained
at www.ICGtesting.com
Printed in the USA
BVHW02n1333161018
530033BV00020B/583/P